BURN THURSDAY

"Poetry, Playlists, and Prayers for Healing"

SYREETA BROWN

Jeanette
I hope that you love my Born Thursday.
There is something for everyone inside of this book.
I appreciate your support and encouragement. You are a beautiful woman.
Love
Syreeta

ISBN: 978-0-578-60780-1

Editor: Laurie Garris
Cover Photography: Porsche Jones
Back Cover Photography: Candace Stewart
Cover Design: Marjorie Law
Jewelry & Accessories:
October Blu, Elena Love, Randy D.

DEDICATION

This book is for you, mama. We always said that we would publish a poetry book. You are the first person who encouraged me to write by buying me composition books and journals. You never read my writings which gave me the freedom to pen my secrets safely. I love you deeply. I know that everything good about my heart comes from you. I watched you struggle and fight my entire life and the struggle continues with your illness now. Regardless, I know that God has been so good to us and he continues to give us time. Our relationship hasn't been the best the last few years, but you are the first person that I loved, and you had my purest heart first. I will always remember the wrestling matches, water fights in the house, 10 cent foot massages, the long hugs and affection, and you telling me that you loved me…all the time. You are the most outrageous-inappropriate person that I know…besides myself. I am so grateful and thankful for you! Your deep love made me comfortable in my own skin.

Most of all, I am thankful that you introduced me to God. You made me get up every Sunday for church. You made sure that we all had a spiritual foundation and that is the greatest gift that you could give a child. It is common for little black girls and little black boys to promise to buy their mamas houses "when they grow up". I promised you a house, and I promised you a book. Here is the book, that I hope will pay for the house. I love you most!

CONTENTS

ACKNOWLEDGMENTS

I would like to acknowledge some valuable people in my life. I could not imagine going through my life without the unconditional support from you all. I apologize, in advance, if I forgot anyone. I could have had a book filled with dedications and acknowledgements. There are more acknowledgements in the back of the book.

Randy, you're the man who inspired me to complete this book. I met you during a time of healing and grief. You propelled me forward in a profound way. I truly now understand the phrase "god send" because of you. You were unexpected but deeply needed and appreciated. Things did not work out the way I had hoped but I am grateful for my season with you. I love you forever!

Thank you to Laurie, my Editor and now beautiful friend. I love your soul. I love your kids. I love that you are always ready and willing to support me in every way. I am grateful for your heart.

Thank you to my children-by blood and by love-Lamont, Victoria, and Otis-thank you for living your best lives and inspiring me to always show up and be the best version of myself. Parenting you three has been the best part of my life, hands down!

Thank you for our outrageous family game nights with all my loves: Brandin, Mel, Marjorie, Vic, Lamont, Otis, Breeze, Toby, and Porsche. I have never played so many versions of Uno or seen so much cheating. Hilarious!

To all the men that I have loved and learned from. I have not written for each of you but my ability to love with depth is because of my experiences with you all. Burn Thursday was started because of a deeply painful uncoupling. But the journey of this book became bigger than Him, bigger than Me, bigger than Us. I dedicate this book to all of the men who made me feel.

Thank you to Porsche, and Victoria who slept over every night until I was able to sleep peacefully.

Thank you to Lamont and Meg who came over for painting, mowing the lawn, and random talks when I hurt.

Thank you to Porsche-my sister, friend, daughter, confidante. Always present and ready to help me in every way. I don't even remember my life without you in it.

Thank you to Papa bear, aka Breeze, for all of our "cocaine" moments, late night talks, day drinking, and Uno Flip. You, being here, made me feel sane, and not alone. I cannot wait to see you on bookshelves, and in the credit of shows. You are an amazing writer, and friend. I love you.

Thank you to my Arizona family-Chuck, Laurynn, baby Chuck, My Rico, aka Paul, Tat, Nicky Poo (aka Nick), Adam, Jamie, and Adam. You guys re-energized me during the last stages of this book with your fuckery. I am my most silly, outrageous self, when I'm with you. I love you, and I love the way that you love me!

Barb, thank you for all of our talks, and silliness as girls and as women. We hold each other's secret hearts and still love each other.

Thank you to my Ina Bear. I would not have gotten through this last year without you. You are my soul sister. You were one of the few people who knew my pain and cried for me. Thank you for the prayers, pep talks and crying sessions. I would not have healed thoroughly without you. I love you!

Thank you for my SOF Fitness Family in Santa Clarita. Part of my sanity was kept intact by my self-care. Thank you, James, for checking in when you didn't see me regularly at the gym. I am so blessed that our gym is a culture of love, forgiveness, and encouragement. I can easily name 30 men and women that I adore working out with, but I will just name a couple-Denice, and Anita, thank you for always keeping me accountable, and for our daily group texts. Thank you, Miss Princess Faith, for cheering us on while we sweat and complain. Thank you to all of the trainers who have contributed to my smaller ass: Howard, Ariel, Jon, Shelby, Carol, Joan, Mike, Shea, Carlos, Claudia, Mariangeles, and James.

A special dedication to my cousin Lakesha, aka-Keke, you protected me when we were on the streets. I didn't even understand the possible things that could have and would have happened to me if you had not been there schooling me constantly. We rarely talk about the past, but I know that I survived because of you. You made me happy and always made sure that we still had kid fun. Ironically, you were the one to teach me about self-care early. You always made sure that our hair was permed and dyed with Kool Aid…my favorite!

To my heart, my confidante and sister Sherry, thank you for checking up on me when my soul "cries out" to you. You always know when I'm hurting, and need you, and vice versa. You hold all my little girl secrets and woman dreams. You have been one of the best things about being on this planet.

Shebur, you are the first person to tell me that you loved my soul. I share the same sentiment towards you. We have always shared loved stories and poetry. *Shebur, Shebur, Shebur, the girl with lots of fur…* I laugh every time I think of our silly poems back and forth to make each other laugh. Your messy is your message, and your tests are your testimonies. I can't wait to read it!

To my siblings-by blood and by love-Quinton, Tamisha, Gabrielle, Sherry, Angie, Chuck, Koko, Jazmyne, and B.J. You are all my first playmates. You taught me how to share, be silly, and how to take care of others. We all survived because of each other's love and attention. All those things gave me the skills that I needed to balance the craziness of our childhood and the shit show of adulthood. I love you deeply!

Thank you, Vanessa, for initiating the conversation that initiated the story that became this book! Our crazy mornings, our ADHD, and random talks. You started this!

FOREWORD

During my life as a speaker, spiritual guide and mentor, I have had the privilege of working with brilliant indigenous elders and some of the great thought leaders of our time. Syreeta Brown's book, *Burn,* has elements of both leaders. She has a way of unapologetically diving deep into troubled waters, yet never suggesting that the reader feel sorry for her. Instead, she helps her audience feel empowered by letting them into her pain,
her process, and her perseverance. She seamlessly employs autobiographical stories and poetry to take the reader on a journey of self-discovery, and in the process, provides a glimpse into her own evolution. In the elegantly executed *Burn,* Syreeta empowers her readers to live authentic lives, and supports them on their path to self-awareness, emotional and sensual awakening.
I have had the opportunity to interview some of the greatest authors in the personal growth field such as, Don Miguel Ruiz, Gregg Bradden, and Marianne Williamson. Syreeta Brown is surely taking her place among them with this book.

Greg Friedman,
Radio Program Host, KX 93.5
Spiritual Guide
International Speaker and Mentor
GregFriedman.com

PREFACE

My most secret place is my heart in print. Once put into words, I seem so small. My weaknesses and most raw self are exposed for your eyes to read as much as you please: my devastation, my brokenness, my strength, and my depth. You search for deep meaning and the secrets hidden in my words, but they're no longer hidden. I am not complex and complicated. I am a simple woman who loves with extra ordinary depth. Once you are in my heart, there is an additional beat for you that is never ending. My love for you creates a life rhythm that is too hard to contain,

so, I write.

Poetry exposes the me that even I don't want to see. A place that no one has been allowed to visit. Burn Thursday is me, inside out. The emotional debit of writing seemed too costly but then I received a deposit of faith and resilience. Don't stare too long, this will be your only glimpse inside of me.

My most important words are the hardest to say,

so, I write.

-Syreeta Brown

I Know Human Matches

"Human Matches are people that show up in your life to set shit on fire, watch you burn, light up everything you hold dear, and/or light a fire under your ass! Sometimes they manage to do them all."

Syreeta Brown

THE SIMMER

CHAPTER 1
INTRODUCTION

I don't remember when I started writing. Honestly, I cannot remember not writing. I will minimize backtracking into my childhood and why I had a social worker, but I had one. Her name was Kathleen. I remember her fondly. She said one of the most life- changing statements to me. During our last session, she sat down right in front of me, and she said, *"Syreeta, you're going to be okay. I'm not worried about you because you write."* She must have sensed the helplessness that reeked off of my preteen body. Or maybe she was just trying to reassure us both. She continued, "*Never stop writing because it allows you to get everything that's going on inside of here, and here, out of you*", as she pointed to her heart and head. Kathleen said that I would survive my childhood because I wrote. My writings were so painfully raw and exposed me so thoroughly that I would survive this world if I kept taking what happening to me and penning it. She said that as long as I wrote, I would be okay I didn't curse as a kid, but I was thinking *"What the fuck does okay mean?" "What does okay feel like?"* I had no idea. This was our last meeting before I was returned to my mother. I was confused, and my anxiety owned me. My obsessive thoughts were spinning me: *I'm surely about to drown in the fuckery of my life and you tell that if I write I will be okay?* Of course, I did not say any of this. It was one of my many fantasy moments where I made up a complete story and dialogue in my ADHD imaginative mind, and played it out. Instead of screaming, crying, or throwing something, I just sat there, a meek, unrecognizable version of the woman I am today, and shook my head in agreement.

Her words have echoed inside of me for the last 30 years. When I asked people who/what is the love of my life, I received mixed answers. The loves of my life are my mom, dancing, God, and writing. Initially, and in that order of introduction.

I grew up the oldest of seven children, five girls, and two boys. My mother started using drugs heavily in her late 20's. It's her story to tell but relevant as to why I started writing. All of my initial writings were about my mama. I wrote about my love for her, my anger towards her. I wrote poetry and short stories, and love letters. I wrote about her drug use. Most of my writings were centered around helplessness, a feeling that I knew and despised. Unfortunately, when I was 14-years old, we had a house fire. I was home by myself with four of my siblings. The house had no gas, or electricity turned on. Everything had been disconnected at the time. We had been sleeping on the porch. My baby brother and I had moved everyone from room to room looking for the origin of the smoke in the air of the house, but we never saw the actual fire. When the smoke was too much, we set up chairs outside, and I fell asleep with my baby sister on my lap. The sound that will haunt me forever was the windows popping out of the house. That's the sound that woke me up. I stood there in an eerie trance. I felt it about to happen again. I had started having out-of-body experiences as a child. I only had them in the moments, that would create the memories, that would haunt me forever. And this was one those moments. I now know that my out-of-body experiences protected me, and removed me partially from the events that could have destroyed me mentally, emotionally, and physically. I watched the fire quickly spread from one side of the house to the other. I saw the flames, so angry, and destructive, leaving nothing untouched. The entire house burned down. God knew that that house had to go. The house, and the street we lived on held so much of the wrong in my life. So many bad things happened in that house. My friend lived across the street, six houses down, until her mother killed her, her siblings, the dog, and then herself because she didn't want to leave them to *"suffer in this world without her."* That was what I had overheard. So, fuck Tampa-the street, and fuck that house!

My eyes stung when I realized the turquoise dress from my Auntie Kathy's wedding was left inside. A dress that I adored because I was a bridesmaid in her wedding, the first wedding I had ever attended. The local news crew arrived before the fire department. I stood in the middle of the street trying to contain the excitement of my three younger sisters and brother, while I watched everything burn. I just stood there in shock. Not yet horrified by the house burning.

When the fire department arrived and started asking questions, I grabbed my brother and sisters and started running down the street. I didn't want my mother to be in trouble or for the police to know we were alone, so we ran…barefoot and barely clothed. It was a hot evening. We didn't even have shoes anymore. We walked away with nothing or maybe we walked away with everything. Although my heart hurt, I still did not cry. I had learned early on not to waste tears. I saved them for when I really needed them. Nothing was saved. I wasn't devastated initially, there was too much other shit to worry about.

My true devastation for my writings came later that summer. I realized that all of my books, journals, writings, and pictures were burned. My mother had kept me supplied with journals, and composition books. She told me that she would never read them because her mother had betrayed her trust, and she wouldn't do that to me. I believed her.

My trust for her allowed me the freedom to write all of my secrets. I don't know if she read them but if she did, she never told one secret.

Writing is what I always turned to when I was hurting. The pain of watching my mother struggle with addiction was managed by getting it out of me and onto paper. The loss of my books and journals cost me emotionally. Regarding poetry, up until the fire I had only written poetry about my mama on drugs. But after the summer of the fire, I never wrote about my mother again.

That summer changed me forever. After the house burned, I spent the summer taking care of my four younger siblings and keeping our secret so we wouldn't be taken from my mother. When August rolled around, I went back to school despite what was going on. I realize that this was the first of a familiar theme of me living a double life and being a fraud in my own life. Most of my friends did not know that during middle school and high school I lived in seven or eight different houses/apartments, a homeless shelter, and at least 15-20 different motels. I couldn't speak about what I saw or what I went through outside of school, so I wrote about it. I wrote so many poems about my mama's struggles like they were my own.

In my sophomore year of high school, I met the second

person that I would primarily write about. He was my saving grace: I fell deeply in love with him. I had my most intimate relationship with him and it did not include sex. We spent most of our time hiding out writing letters, poetry, and thoughts back and forth during the school day. He changed my writings. Up until then all of my writings were dark and sad. When I started writing again, because of him, all of my poetry was about falling in love, discovering intimacy and learning about myself as a sensual being. During the day I was at peace and distracted, and after school, he and I would sit on the phone until one of us fell asleep or one of our mothers screamed, *"Stop making love on that damn phone."* This boy later became the man who initially inspired this book.

I have three beautiful children, whom I adore and cherish. My eyes water when I think of them, yet I haven't written about them. I hadn't written about motherhood, dance, and/or all the other things and people who have touched me, just my mother, and a few men.

Now… 29 years later.

My co-worker Vanessa came into my office in February of this year and we started having a random conversation (as we often do) and she mentioned “The Moth." Of course, my AHDH, haha, ADHD is immediately intrigued. “The Moth” turned out to be a story slam showcase in DTLA. As cited on their Wikipedia, *“The Moth is a non-profit group based in New York City dedicated to the art and craft of storytelling. Founded in 1997, the organization presents a wide range of theme-based storytelling events across the United States and abroad, often featuring prominent literary and cultural personalities.”* They have monthly topics, and you can enter your name into a lottery to be selected to tell your story in five minutes. The topic for the month was "Love Hurts." Hell, yes it does! I was ready to write my story, but I realized that I could not attend because of a meeting. So, I looked for the next showcase title. April's theme was "Burn." My heart started pounding fast. That's it! Burn, I know about burn. I knew and had loved human matches. I had recently gone through a breakup that had changed the very breath that I took. I was scared shitless of attending the Moth but the need to release the pain made me brave enough to start writing a short story to possibly present. I have been open about my life, but my poetry had always been a private part of me. Dancing was the way I put my emotions into movement, and I had no problem expressing myself through movement. But my words, written or spoken out loud, could never be taken back. I had attended a plethora of slams, shows, open mics, but I had never gotten up to speak my most private self. To this day, I have not been on the mic.

This book is because of Kathleen's words "*You're going to be okay Syreeta. I'm not worried about you because you write. Never stop writing because writing allows you to get everything that's going on inside of here and here out of you."* When my last coupling ended, I was not okay. I was deeply attached to a Human Match. I knew and loved him deeply. Initially this book was about my grief, and processing of that relationship-through poetry. But as I started writing I was forced to look at all of my couplings and myself as a deeply wounded person. After much self-regulation, and thought I realized that many of my wounds were self-inflicted. Through writing, I realized how careless I had been with myself.

My ex came into my life and set shit on fire. Initially the burn was good. I felt a depth of emotions for another human being that was different than anything I had ever felt before. I made love like I was a human aphrodisiac. Every time we touched it was like I was on ecstasy. I was overly sensitive to his words, his touch, even the way he looked at me. I also, for the first time had no boundaries with a man. Let me rephrase that: I have always had boundaries, but in this coupling, my boundaries burned- one by one. I watched them burn. I realized that I had a history of making up excuses and giving passes for the men in my life. I allowed anyone into my space. I always stayed and played because of the possibilities. Not understanding the liabilities of giving myself so freely to others left me vulnerable. I had no idea the cost and expense of loving him in particular. I left that relationship completely poor. I felt robbed of all things that I held dear. I was angry, ashamed, embarrassed, and devastated. I recognized sadness and despair for the first time. I was grieving like I had suffered a death. I realize now that I had suffered a loss and I was grieving. He and I had a full life that appeared to be rich. But now I cannot even know him. I thought I would never breathe the same because of the loss.

In retrospect he didn't burn me nor did the others. I burned myself. I saw the matches and knew the ending to each of my stories with them. I took no precautions to protect myself when I felt that men of the past were careless with me. My Burners are not horrible people. Hurt people unfortunately hurt people. And that lesson also applied to me. I was also a Human Match.

The opening of this book is very different than the end of it. I have experienced a new version of myself through my grieving and self-care.

"Burn Thursday" is not some life-changing read, or even my best work. This poetry book contains poems that range from juvenile to intense, passages and prayers that I wrote to get through the days, and playlists that I listened to drown my pain and uplift my spirit when I needed to. I don't have a writing style. When something is on my heart, I sit down and get it out of me. I don't try and rhyme it or check for grammar. There are a few intentional things that I did to move through my pain. This poetry book is one of them.

Although I have other writings to publish, I always thought

my first publication should be a poetry book. Poetry and Dance are my babies. I've spent my entire life "dancing it out." Now is the time to write it out. "Burn Thursday" is my self-indulgent closure to a love that ended tragically, reflections of loves of the past, and the beginning of flowers blooming on new love. More than anything, writing "Burn Thursday" was the healing that I needed to be okay.

There are three types of burns:

- First-degree burns damage only the outer layer of skin
- Second-degree burns damage the outer layer and the layer underneath
- Third-degree burns damage or destroy the deepest layer of skin and tissues underneath

CHAPTER 2
POEMS
FIRST DEGREE BURNS

Listen

When He Said

I was too much

He meant that

He was not Enough

He Knew

Pride

You told me that

You needed me…

One time

Then you started

Punishing the both of us

Bitter Love Tragedy?

You are and have always been my weakness

You challenge me in a way that is foreign to me

I have been bound by my strong sense of right and wrong

Never living in the moment

Always thinking about the consequences

You make me want to throw it to the wind

To run away with you and never look back

How do we change this from a Bitter Love Tragedy?

There are countless books, songs, and sonnets about us

We Are who true lovers look up to

People are drawn to use as examples

My gut feelings tell me that you are my forever

That I could easily lose myself to you

I am flooded by my overwhelming love for you

It's been halfway because of us

No more walking towards each other, start running

Have mercy on me

Please

Understand my desire is not to create a tornado

As I plow through the debris of my life

If you believe in dreams, and I know that you do

Remember that… You are my Romeo

And I have always been your Juliet

Our story doesn't end with you tucked under my pillow

It ends with my head tucked under your head

My hand over your heart

Your hand over my hand

Whispers and pillow talk

In reality, this is not a Bitter Love Tragedy

It's just a very long love story

Mine (Call and Response)

You have consumed my thoughts.

My passion for you appeared to be contained

but was only sedated.

I am fully charged and so raw

exposed by my love for you.

Now I'm awake and I can't let you go not to anyone.

I don't want to know about her because

You are mine

You have always been.

And I am yours

It's you that I belong to

Everyone sees when you look at me.

Everyone knows when I look at you

We only fool ourselves

Trying to function half of a whole

There is no chase…catch me

The Victims of Unsynchronized Passion

It's hard for my heart when I talk to you

I feel at home, a peace and surrender

Why does my stomach get butterflies when I think of you?

Why does my mind wander to thoughts of you?

Why am not able to move on?

I'm stuck in a time period when things were so simple

Feelings were so pure

smiles came too easy

It's hard for my heart when I talk to you

I feel at home a peace and surrender

Is not mine to have

I belong to someone else

Yet

Why does my stomach get butterflies when I think of you?

Why does my mind wander to thoughts of you?

Why am I unable to let you be my past?

I Wonder

I wonder what it would feel like to be free to be...with you

To hold your hands in the store

To kiss you every time you look at me

What would it be like to be your girlfriend?

To touch you as I please?

What would it feel like to call you mine?

To know that you were mine to please

to tease

to have?

I wonder what it would be like to cuddle and watch movies with you

For you to not control your emotions and feelings for me

To take a shower and kiss

...as much as I wanted

To wrap my hands around your waist

and lay my head on your back

I wonder what it would be like to make out

to kiss your neck, rub your head

to tease you with my mouth

To take a trip and hold your hand while you drive

What would it be like to know that you were mine

and never share you again

Do you wonder too?

Hang Up First

Why can't I hang up first?

The sound of your voice

Has me grinning from ear to ear

I can't hang up first

I've tried, but it seems wrong

To disconnect us

So, I stay on

And listen to you breathing

Knowing the silent sound

Of your blush

Please don't make me hang up first

I won't

I'd rather stay in the warmth

Of my feelings for you

I'd rather get the chills

From the sound of you

I want to remain in this peaceful place

And not hang up first

Count to three and we’ll hang up together

1, 2, 3

Damn, that didn't work

I want to talk to you forever

Untitled #1

When I looked at him

I saw all of him

When he looked at me

It was straight through

He had no desire

To honor

No integrity

To just walk away

Instead he stayed

And played

With my heart and life

RAW

I feel raw when I hear your voice

I feel exposed by your tone

I am painfully open to your inflection

I am sensitive to the sound of you

I feel raw

Like

I can never really be prepared

For the feeling of being in my own skin

with you

BEST FRIEND

You were my best friend

You sometimes introduced me to my own skin

I met Fela through you

Believed in Obama because of you

Understood that it was time to go natural

because of you

Parts of Us were so sweet

But the other parts hurt

Why didn’t you show up for me?

CHAPTER 3
POEMS
SECOND DEGREE BURNS

DETOX

I need you

Out

Of

Me

I need to be cleansed

I

Can't

Keep

You

You are not for my spirit

You

Contaminate

Me

I need you

Out Of Me

USB DRIVE

Today I put our life on a USB drive

3500 pictures

608 videos

I couldn't stop looking at your face and smiles

I knew them all

I looked at each picture to see how you were feeling

And then I saw the truth

After I was done, I sat on the bed for hours and cried

So painful I turned the volume up on the tv

I couldn't bear the sound of my crying

Letting you go

Was the hardest to do

But I know that it is right

For me and you

I will forever sting

When I hear your name

And my heart will burn

Because I never thought

I would have to give you up

But

Letting you go was the right thing to do

You broke my heart

And every time I see you

It's like pouring alcohol on an open wound

You were careless with me

As time goes on

I will heal

But I will never be open for you again

I took no precautions loving you

I hope we have both learned a lesson

Because the loss of our friendship

Was the sacrifice and consequence

Vulnerable

You're the only man

That has ever had a hold over me.

I feel attachment and emotions untapped by others

Instead of feeling exhilarated and free

I feel scared and alone

Not secure in the reciprocation of those needs

I kept my feet planted but now I want to flee

I don't want to be this open and raw with anyone

I am drawn to you but too exposed to ever follow through

I feel as though I am running, and you are walking

You are silent while I am talking

I am expressive, while you are repressive

I over analyze

While you simplify my complex feelings

I am left feeling a little disappointed with our exchanges

So, I am setting comfortable boundaries for myself

Today I decided I am going to fall out of love with you

you don't need it, or don't deserve it

I'm not sure which of the two

But I am no longer going to be consumed by you

You had the part of me that mattered the most…my heart

I accepted pieces of you

You spent our time showing me you weren't invested

You didn't say or do anything

To give me false hopes

Making excuses and seeing the possibilities

Not the liabilities of giving

Myself to you

But I will fall out of love with you

And when I am weak

I will pull out my list

Of why we will never be

I will remind myself

Of how you tried to break me

I left myself vulnerable

WHEN I WAS DONE

when I was done

I asked god for help

because I knew

I could never leave on my own

So I prayed for you to be removed

I prayed for me to be able to breath

I prayed

and I prayed

and I PRAYED

and I PRAYED

and I PRAYED

and I PRAYED

and I PRAYED

and I P R A Y E D

Then you were removed

and my sanity stayed in your place

YOU WE US

I

felt

every

emotion

of

them

Even

above

my

own

You We Us

AM I YOUR CUP OF TEA?

All Heart not Much Else

I'm all heart

If nothing more

I pour

All of me into all you

And spill out

I don't know how to stay in the cup

I always overflow

I am all hot or all cold

I cannot be lukewarm

I try to balance

BUT

I'm all heart

If nothing more

I feel deep

And love hysterically

It is without control

I do

I try but cannot deny

When my emotions feel

I pour

All of me into all you

And spill out

I don't know how to stay in the cup

So, I always overflow

I am all hot or all cold

I cannot be lukewarm

I try to balance

But....

I want you

To drink all of me

MI AMOR

You hurt me

you dismissed what is most important to me

Words

Untitled #2

You Hurt Me

You Hurt HeL

You Hurt HeD

You Hurt HeY

You Hurt HeR

YOU ARE NOT SAFE TO LOVE

you are not safe to love

you take my love and throw it about

never understanding the gift you receive

you think i love lightly?

most cannot handle a portion of my depth

but i gave it to you

while you gave to others

Bad

I wanted you so bad

So, I gave myself up

Over

And

Over

And

Over

And

Over

And

Over

And

Over

And

Over

and over and over and over and over

Again

CHAPTER 4
POEMS
THIRD DEGREE BURNS

So Easy

Why was it so Easy

For you to Fuck Her?

And her

And her

And her

And her

And her

And her

And her

And her

And her

And her

Why was It So Easy?

Because I Stayed

Untitled #3

When I found out you fucked her

I wasn’t even hurt

I was mad

bully

You must be confused if you thought

I would stay unglued

I am not amused

your misconduct I refuse

You have no Clue that you will Lose

This battle that you Choose

What will you do now that I don’t have the Blues?

You are Excused!

I’m a Fucking Boss

I thought you knew

SQUATTER

I am not a temporary place to be
we do not throw things on floors
we put them on shelves

I am not a temporary shelter to stay
you do not shit where you sleep
you are a man not a pet

I Am Home

I am not a temporary place to sleep
I feel deep
I am whipped shea butter
honey and tea

I am not a hangout
I diffuse and refuse
to be used by you

I Am Home

I am not a vacation
do not pretend to miss me
while you kiss on others

I am not a...
I am not a cot for you to rot
I am bamboo pillows and downy filled duvets

I Am Home

I light and love
I am your calm and peace
not a side chick for your community dick

IMPOSTER

You tried

but you could never hide

I saw you

All of you

Even the part you thought was a secret

IMPOSTER

But I loved him too

When I met him he was prideful but seductive

he often spoke like a knife

Using his tongue to slice

He was deceitful but nice

You spoke of love

Followed by "Fuck you"

You stood in my face

With the appearance of grace

As you cut me emotionally

you spoke of your deep passion

But you were an emotional assassin

A lover of no one but yourself

IMPOSTER

A liar and cheater

A mental beater

You were mean and used your tongue to cut my spirit

A coward and fake

You pretended to lift me high

So that you could drop me hard

I thought you were funny and confident

But only cowards laugh at others

Fake smiles to distract

As you tore from the back

Spreading yourself

To hide that you're not whole

IMPOSTER

Imposter cont…

Manipulations and lies

With pen you speak highly of us

But it's just to get a hold

So, you can fuck us with nice words

You tried

but you could never hide

I saw you

All of you

Even the part you thought was a secret

IMPOSTER,

but I loved him too

PTSD

You Often treated our relationship like trauma

Perpetually having an out of body experience

You tried to be present but safely kept yourself hidden away.

You never preferred our coupling over your desire to protect yourself with solitude.

You placed additional blankets of pride and ego to protect yourself from a storm that was never coming.

I was not the tornado that swept us up

It was you

In the Shower

I cried

Everyday

knowing

I should leave

But asking god

For a little more time

To suffer with you

SUFFOCATE

I am able to take deeper breaths

Because we don’t share oxygen

any longer

Me Too

Inside

Of

Me

Without

My

Permission

Groggy

Dry

No

Inside

Of

Me

Without

My

Permission

Groggy

Dry

No

BURN THURSDAY

Inside

Of

Me

Without

My

Permission

Groggy

Dry

No

I SAID NO

I SAID NO

I SAID NO

I SAID NO

I SAID NO

I SAID NO

I SAID NO

I SAID NO

I SAID NO

Not the Drink

Your addiction consumed us
She loved you differently than me
She gave you immediate highs
And crashed you down low

She didn't pace herself with you

She was seductive
I was unable to satisfy you anymore
She took away your pain
Gave you the numbness that you needed to get by

She kept calling you back to her

But I couldn't compete with her
Thorough hold on you
She owned you in every way
You tried to let her go

I tried to stay

Your mood swings were unbearable
I had seen this before
You were my mama all over again
But this time I had a choice

We had them so I could not to stay

Pray First

I talked to god today

He said that he didn't know you

I wish I had prayed sooner

Then I would have known

Untitled #4

Close your eyes

You see to fucking much

Of me

Mad

Today

I
give
zero
fucks
about
You

Today

FOOLISH

I don't want to think of anyone else when I feel bound to us

He tells me that I'm the one for him

When I feel I was made for you

I catch him looking at me

While I'm thinking of you

He tries to comfort me

When you created my tears

He is chasing me

As I go after you

I am complimented and adored

But I want that from you

I cannot be touched or kissed

By anyone but you

There is no way for me to fall in love with him

When I'm deeply in love with you

LET ME GO

I keep trying to come up with ways

To really let you go

But you do just enough

To keep me hanging on

Sometimes you give me

Just a glimpse of what could be

And I am left confused

How could you not fight for me?

I have no self-control

I'm just waiting for you

To let me go

But

You

Don't

And I'm left wondering why

When you do so little to keep me

CHAPTER 5
POEMS
SLOW BURNS

Untitled #5

I'm not much on porn
Not when I know the power of my mind
I can grind

I can kiss
I can fuck
I can suck

I can lick
I can touch
I know how much

I can feel what you need
By the breaths you take
I watch you squirm

I'm not much on porn
Not when I know the magic between ears

I can ride
I can bend
I know when

I determine how fast
I control how slow
I Am
Thorough

Leaving no part of you untouched

YOU, INSIDE OF ME

You inside of me

Is something I want forever

My body trembles when you first enter me

The tip of you wets me

And I can feel every inch of you slide

Inside of me

My heart beats fast

Because I know the next sound Will be you...

Ummm…I love you, you whisper

"I love you too...so much"

then the energy changes

I hold you hostage

inside of me

I arch to join the rhythm

Of you

But you slide out until

just the Tip is haunting me

Teasing me

You feel so damn good

I'm constantly contracting because

You

Make

Me

Pant

For

You

You handle me completely

You know that I need you back inside of me

But you make me wait

Because I will

Always

Because...you inside of me

Is...

ADDICT

I am trying to kick this habit

Trying to sleep at night

But looking for a fix

Having physical withdrawals

Getting the shakes

The injection of your erection

Was just too much

You shot fire in me

now I am roaming

looking for a fix

If I’m not thinking about it

I'm wanting it

Craving it

Just needing

Another injection

Hoping you will help

Can you please help me?

Inject

Your

Infectious

Genital love

Into my vaginal cove

Please

Fix me

Lick me

Stop this shaking

I need you

You are making it impossible to kick this habit of you

Please give me a fix

I am an Addict

You Are

Sexy sensual

Occupying plenty of my thoughts

Keeps me aching for your touch

I know how your hands feel on my skin

And it makes it impossible to concentrate

How am I supposed to be productive

When I feel your tongue on my neck

Your fingers between my legs?

How should I proceed with my greed of you?

Should I lift up so you can enter me?

Or stay still and wait

IMPOSSIBLE

I want to rise to the occasion

I want to help you get inside of me

QUICK

I am panting and breathing heavy

I can hear the sound of my heart

beating against your chest

Let that set the pace of your rhythm

Bump bump

Bump bump

Bump bump

Don't make me wait

I can feel your heart beat inside of me

You’re stealing my pulse with every stroke

You are wearing me out

Tantric

Floor
Pillow
Naked
Leg wrap

Breath

My arms
Your legs
Your feet
My cheeks

Breath…

Head back
Hips rock
You lean
I scream

Hold it
Breath…

My arms
Your legs
Your feet
My cheeks

Head back
Hips rock
You lean

I scream

Hold it
Breath…

FUCKed by You (Fuck Trilogy #1)

What's a girl to do

when all she wants is to be fucked by you?

I can play pretty and be shy but why

when all I want are your hands on my thighs?

Touch me

Brush your tongue across my lips

enter my world orally

Stick your hands inside my pants

make me pant

The tip of your finger

Makes me wet

How do I taste?

What's a girl to do

When all she wants is to be fucked by you?

Don't worry about shedding my clothes

Fuck that, make my body glow

FUCK IT OUT (Fuck Trilogy #2)

Why can't we just fuck it out?

I need to be cleansed of this craving of you

I need to release it through an orgasm

Created by you

Kiss me

On my lips

I want to feel you

Come close

I want to feel your breath on my face

Stick your tongue out I'll meet you halfway

Umm

You taste good in my mouth

If we're going to fuck it out

Look at me

I'm not laying on my back

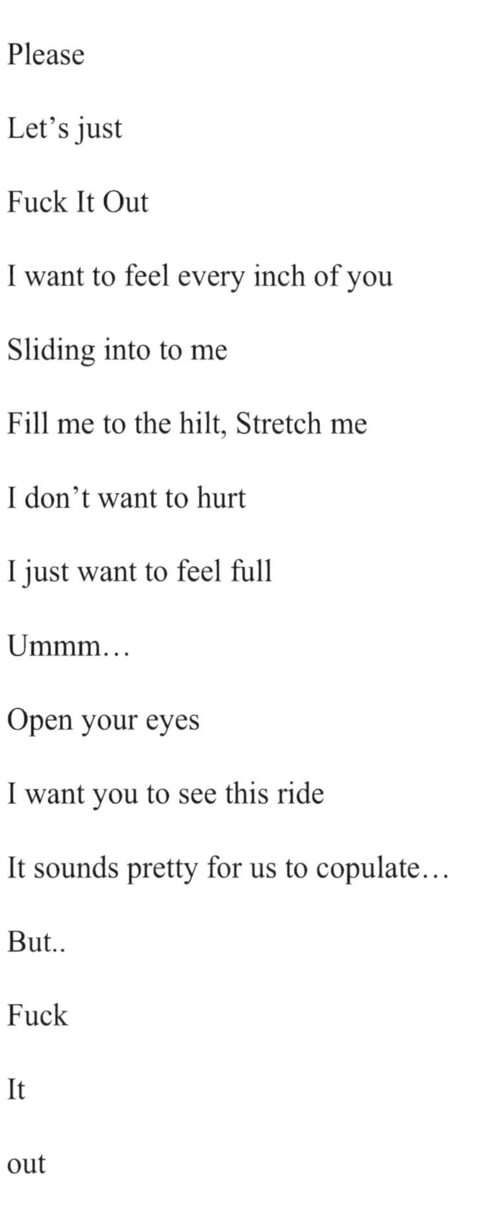

Please

Let's just

Fuck It Out

I want to feel every inch of you

Sliding into to me

Fill me to the hilt, Stretch me

I don't want to hurt

I just want to feel full

Ummm…

Open your eyes

I want you to see this ride

It sounds pretty for us to copulate…

But..

Fuck

It

out

FUCK (Fuck Trilogy #3)

Fuck

You are achingly beautiful

I am committed to loving you forever

Not because it's easy

But because I have no choice

You hold my heart

I am terribly in love with you

There are too many minutes in a day

Too many hours spent on you

I am trying not ache for you

I am trying

But…

Fuck…

You are achingly beautiful

I am committed to loving you forever

Not because it’s easy

But because I have no choice

You are my heart

Fuck

You are achingly beautiful

I am committed to loving you forever

Not because it’s easy

But because I have no choice

You have my heart

I Like The Way You Kiss Her

I like the way you kiss her
I'm your drug you say
But I'm in need of a fix…I crave you

I want to squeeze your head
Between my legs
And shake uncontrollably

You love kissing her
So, you make me watch
You want to own her

I want you please…just kiss her
Your tongue consumes me
You knew this would happen

She throbs when you're near
I'm your drug you say
But I'm in need of a fix

Why do you devour her
With open mouthed kisses
Because you know

Another injection
Of your oral affection

Might be too much

CHAPTER 6
THE SALVE

SoulSmile

Every nerve ending comes alive

when I walk into the studio.

The floors

The mirrors

The bars

They awake a part of me

that will never be dormant

Once the music is added

My eyes close

My body

starts to move

For a moment I know

My soul can smile

Dance

Hopeful

I am a hopeful romantic.

The kind of woman that expects grand gestures from a man who says he wants to spend his life with me.

I'm dynamic but simple.

I love affectionate hugs that last until we are both satisfied.

Deep long kisses that end in mutual sighs.

Most of all, I love to hear you express his love for me

with words.

Not because I am needy but because I deserve to hear how much you care about me.

I expect all of these things

because they will be given back in abundance.

I'm Hopeful!

I,

a woman who has depth and wisdom

I am choosing a man who has presence when he steps in a room.

Who has a smile that lights up my space.

Who has a touch that brings my body calmness.

Loving me is not for the faint at heart.

I am strong willed.

I am direct and assertive.

I am a feminist with a mama bear's heart.

But with the right man

I am challenged to see my wrongness

appreciated for my rightness

respected for my stillness.

You will want to pray for me

and honor our coupling

You will be transparent

You will always fight for me,

for We

I Apologize

I apologize to all of the women

That I have said

Be strong

You're too good for him

You will find better

You deserve better

Be brave

You don't need him

Don't waste your tears

Fuck those clichés

I apologize

I should have said

Let me hold you

You are worthy

Find yourself

Honor yourself in all things

You inspire me -Trust God- Cry it out

Deep Sigh

I won't say he completes me

We are already whole

He is the truth

A true reflection of my deep passion

He challenges my emotions

I am hyper aware of being a woman

I am more sensitive and vulnerable in his presence

There is this deep sense of calm and rightness when we touch

I am a better version of myself through his love

When I see him look at me

It's a mirror image of what I feel for him reflecting back

We are not without faults and challenges

But I am dedicated to him, to Us

Our passion is sometimes too intense

So, we are stepping back

We have to remember what is most important-

Our ego and pride?

Or our undeniable chemical draw to spend our life together?

I choose the latter each time

We have been without the other

We were imbalanced

He holds my peace

I hold his harmony

He is my language of love

He is the mate to my soul

He is the universe's reflection of me

I love him deeply

He is my Deep Sigh

God Send

I met this man

He talks to my soul

My spirit comes alive at the sound of his voice

He speaks to me the way God intended

He knows me

The me that others don't see

He understands my purpose and gifts

He loves my wild hair

And adores my smiles

He thinks I am hasty with my emotions

And loud in speech

But that's debris from the past

As long as he is patient

He will be rewarded with my gifts

And my Light

I know that his presence

Is no accident

Or coincidence

He is here to propel me

To show me what a thriving woman looks like

His words stop me
Make me accountable
And present…to God, to Me, to Him
He says that there is
Nothing between us
Not even air

He is transparent
Because God knew what I needed
He says that he is a Soldier
And soldiers never leave their post

He lets me know him
…sometimes
He too has to open more for me
But I am watching him try
and loving me some of him

I Hate Her

she feels every emotion
of others
it is often too much

SOMETIMES I HATE HER

she is the weakest part of me
My Anxiety

she shows up
whenever she pleases
no respect
for my fragility

she makes me cry
i am ashamed of her
because she knows
i am broken

SOMETIMES I HATE HER

I have more control over her now
but she always lingers
waiting for me to hurt again
so she can come through

she is the weakest part of me
her name is anxiety

her ability to make me feel weak
also empowers me
because i know who she is

so today I told her
to fuck off
I don't need her anymore

she was the weakest part of me
her name was anxiety
but I killed her

Today I cried when I went to visit you
It never fails
I’m so in love with you

Barnes and Noble

Breath

You're the reason why
I took a deep breath again
You move the parts of me that have not had oxygen

You replenish my spirit
Refill my peace
And refuel my soul

I am whole
Now it is easier
To accept your presence

Loved

I am loved

I am loved

I am loved

By You

I am loved

I am loved

I am loved

By You

Thank you God

Woman

I am a woman
of the earth
I breed
of the air
I breathe
on the ground
I pray

I am a woman
who loves
who cries
who scream if need be

I am a woman
strong by default
meek to please
leader by nature

Untitled #6

Life is not about transition, it's about movement.

We are ever evolving and in a state of movement.

Transition insinuates waiting for something to happen.

Allow yourself the freedom of movement.

Move through your life knowing that the journey is open.

You can move forward or moved backwards.

But know that you can control the movements.

Move forward and only look back to see the journey

CHAPTER 7
PLAYLISTS

My top 10 Playlists that I listened to this year.

1. Burn
2. Salve
3. Reggae Essentials
4. I Love God
5. Slow Burn
6. Lerner New York
7. Loving Hearts
8. Around The World
9. This Was Us

Burn (exactly what it sounds like)

1. Eminem ft Rihanna. "Love The Way You Lie" *Recovery,* 2010.
2. Gallant ft Jhene Aiko. "Skipping Stones" *Ology,* 2016
3. Sinead Harnett ft Gallant "Pulling Away" *Pulling Away,* 2019
4. Tracy Chapman "Smoke and Ashes" *New Beginning,* 1995
5. Art of Noise "Moments In Love" *In To Battle With The Art Of Noise,* 1983
6. Labrinth "Jealous" *Jealous*, 2014
7. Ella Mai "Naked" *Ella Mai,* 2018
8. Meshell Ndegeocello "Bitter" *Bitter,* 1999
9. Alanis Morissette "You Oughta Know" *Jagged Little Pill,* 1995
10. Meshell Ndegeocello "Fool of Me" *Bitter,* 1999
11. Emeli Sande "Clown" *Our Version Of Events,* 2012
12. Bonnie Raitt "I Can't Make You Love Me" *Luck of the Draw,*1991
13. R.E.M. "Everybody Hurts" *Every hurts,* 1993

Salve (my soothers and empowerment)

1. Labrinth "Let The Sun Shine" *Let the sun shine,* 2010
2. Nico & Vinz "Am I Wrong" *Am I Wrong,* 2013
3. Chaka Khan "Through The Fire" *I Feel for You,* 1984
4. Elton John "I'm Still Standing" *Too Low for Zero, 1982*
5. Toni Braxton "Let It Flow" S*ecrets, 1996*
6. Hailee Steinfield "Love Myself" *Jem and the Holograms,* 2015
7. Sara Bareilles "Brave" *The Blessed Unrest,* 2013
8. Mary J. Blige "Just Fine" *Growing pains,* 2017
9. Maroon 5 "Sugar" *V, 2014*
10. Francis and the Lights "May I Have This Dance" Farewell, Starlite!, 2016

Reggae Essentials

Not just reggae. This list has reggaeton, Caribbean, African, Soca, and Island specific songs. Whenever I listen to this playlist, I feel like traveling and dancing dirty haha. It reminds me of my trip to Belize.

1. Mavado "Tumping" *Dancehallrock*, 2011
2. A-Star "Balaya" *Balaya, 2019*
3. Busy Signal "Stay So" *say so,* 2017
4. Laro "Lovers License" *The Best of Laro,* 1996
5. Laro "Corn Plum Plum" *The Best of Laro,* 1996
6. Blackfacenaija "African Queen" *African Queen, 2008*
7. Tekno "Pano" *Pana, 2016*
8. Agege Tekno "Agege" *Agege, 2019*
9. Etana "Warrior Love" *The strong one,* 2008
10. Richie Spice "Brown Skin" *In the streets of Africa, 2007*
11. 2baba "African Queen" *Face 2 Face,* 2004

I Love God

My spiritual songs that have helped me take deep breaths.

1. Tasha Cobbs "Gracefully Broken" *Gracefully Broken,* 2017
2. Tasha Cobbs "For Your Glory" *Grace*, 2013
3. Michael W. Smith "This Is How I Fight My Battles" *Surrounded,* 2018
4. Christy Nockels "The Air I Breathe" *Passion: One Day Live,* 2000
5. Michael W. Smith "Above All" *Worship,* 2001
6. Anthony Evans "See You Again" *Back to life,* 2017
7. Hezekiah Walker "Every Praise" *Every Praise,* 2013
8. Mary Mary "Shackles" *Thankful,* 2000
9. Fred Hammond "No Weapon" *spirit of David,* 1996
10. JJ Hairston & Youthful Praise "You Deserve It" *You Deserve It, 2016*

11. Tasha Cobbs ft. Kierra Sheard "Your Spirit" *Your Spirit,* 2017
12. Smokie Norful "I Need you Now" *I Need you Now,* 2002
13. Jonathan McReynolds "God is Good" *Make More Room,* 2018
14. VaShawn Mitchell "Nobody Greater" *Triumphant,* 2010
15. Tamela Mann "Take Me To The King" *Best Days, 2017*

Slow Burn

1. Marian Hill "Whisky" *Sway,* 2015
2. Marian Hill "Lips" *Sway,* 2015
3. Rini "Lay You Down" *Rini,* 2017
4. Jeff Bernat "Birthday Suit" *Afterwords,* 2017
5. Rini "Aphrodite" *After the Sun,* 2018
6. Ro James "(All Day I) A.D.I.D.A.S." 2016
7. Rini "Emerald" *Emerald,* 2017
8. Ro James "Permission" *Permission,* 2015
9. Rihanna "Love On The Brain" *Anti,* 2016
10. Marsha Ambrosius "Your Hands" *Late Nights & Early Mornings,* 2011
11. Luke James "These Arms" *These Arms,* 2018
12. Cautious Clay "Cold War" *Cold War Stripped, 2017*
13. Sade Adu "Cherish the Day" 2012
14. Jill Scott "Jahraymecofasola" *Woman,* 2015

Lerner New York

Songs that remind me of being 18-years old and working at Lerner's New York retail store in Panorama City Mall. The store had an 8 track that looped the same songs over during my shift. Sentimental songs.

1. Babyface "It's No Crime" *Tender Lover,* 1989
2. Billy Joel "Uptown Girl" *An Innocent Man, 1983*
3. Billy Joel "Tell Her About It" *An Innocent Man, 1983*
4. Billy Ocean "Caribbean Queen" *Suddenly, 1984*
5. Simply Red "Say You Love Me" *Blue,* 1998
6. Simply Red "Stars" *Blue,* 1998
7. Fleetwood Mac "Dreams" *Rumours,* 1977
8. Simply Red "Sunrise" *Blue,* 1998
9. Shanice "I Love Your Smile" *Inner Child,* 1991
10. Bobby Caldwell "What You Won't Do For Love" *Bobby Caldwell,* 1978
11. Eric Clapton "Tears In Heaven" *Rush,* 1992
12. Chris Isaak "Wicked Game" *Heart Shaped World,* 1989

Loving Hearts

- Created by a man I recently was involved with, and myself. We sent each other song dedications: one of the most mixed genre lists.

1. Roy C "I'm Falling In Love Again" S*ex & Soul,* 1998
2. Sade "The Moon and the Sky" *Soldier of love, 2010*
3. Gallant "Gentleman" *Gentleman,* 2018
4. Ricky Martin "Perdido Sin Ti" *Vuelve, 1998*
5. The Bangles "Eternal Flames" *Everything,* 1988
6. Bob Marley "Turn Your Lights Down Low" *Exodus,* 1977
7. Toby Keith "You Shouldn't Kiss Me Like This" *How Do You Like Me Now,* 1999
8. Sizzla "She's So Loving" *Da Real Thing,* 2002
9. Otis Redding "That's How Strong My Love Is" *The Great Otis Redding Sings Soul Ballards,* 1965
10. Indie Arie "Moved by You" S*ongversation,* 2013

11. James Blunt "You're Beautiful" *Back to Bedlam,* 2004
12. 2baba "African Queen" *Face 2 Face,* 2004
13. Toni Braxton "I Love Me Some of Him" *Secrets, 1996*

Around The World

My top songs that I use when I am teaching my dance class, "Around the World in 60 Minutes".

1. Habib Koite & Bamada "Din Din Wo" *Muso Ko, 1995*
2. Dominique Cerejo "Dhoom Again" *Dhoom:2*, 2006
3. Antibalas "Che Che Cole" *Government Magic,* 2005
4. Honey Singh "Sunny Sunny" *Yaariyan*, 2013
5. Sultan Nooran "Patakha Guddi" *Highway,* 2014
6. Zap Mama "Supermoon" *Supermoon,* 2007
7. Lizzo ft Missy Elliott "Tempo" *Tempo, 2019*
8. Tekno & Zlatan "Agege" *Agege, 2019*
9. Sarina Jain "Masala Bhangra" 2007
10. Sade "The Moon and the Sky" *Soldier of love, 2010*
11. Enrique Iglesias "Bailando" *Bailando Remixes, 2013*
12. A-Star "Balaya" *Balaya, 2019*
13. Mary J. Blige "Just Fine" *Growing pains, 2007*

14. Harry Belafonte "Jump In the Line" *Harry Belafonte's Greatest hits, 1961*
15. Blanco Brown "The Git Up" *The Git Up,* 2019

This Was Us

Playlist that reminded me of my last coupling.

1. India Arie "Beautiful Surprise" *Voyage to India,* 2002
2. India Arie "Purify Me" *Tyler Perry's Diary of a Mad Black Woman*, 2005
3. Indie Arie "Moved by You" S*ongversation,* 2013
4. Ro James "Permission" *Permission,* 2015
5. Lauryn Hill "Just Like Water" *MTV Unplugged No. 2.0,* 2002
6. Jill Scott "Jahraymecofasola" *Woman,* 2015
7. Jeffrey Osbourne "Greatest Love Affair" *Stay With Me Tonight,* 1983
8. Christina Perri "A Thousand Years" *The Twilight Saga: Breaking Dawn pt 1,* 2011
9. James Bay "Let It Go" *Let It Go,* 2014
10. Major "Why I Love You" 2017
11. Miley Cyrus "Wrecking Ball" *Wrecking Ball, 2013*
12. New Edition "Can You Stand the Rain" *Heart Break, 1988*

CHAPTER 8
PRAYERS

This chapter was the most important for my healing. People that know my story always ask me *"Why are you so positive?" How do you smile?" "How do you make it through?"* My answer is that I pray, and that I curse. I am trying to curb the latter. Honestly, I want to get as good at praying as I am at cursing. Cursing flows out of me freely, with passion, and with ease. It's instant and immediately releases my tension. I want that for my prayer life. I want God first. I want to pray every day, most of the day. During my writing of this book, I would pick a couple of days per week to fast, and to focus on praying for others. I set my alarm to go off every hour and I would pray. I would pray for my kids, my co-workers, people that I encountered, my gym loves, my mama, my sisters, my brother, my nieces and nephew, my neighbors, my friends, Mi Amor, my exes. I prayed for everyone. My prayer days were my most productive days. I was so accountable. I believe in God and I believe in praying. I am spiritually driven. These are some of the prayers that I posted on my facebook page during the year. I loved reading my friends "Amens", and prayers that they sent back. The public prayers were healing and needed. Hopefully the prayers will be healing for you too.

Prayer of the Day

Creator, I am working on my spiritual immaturity. My prayers have become routine instead of raw and vulnerable. Without the rawness and vulnerability there is no growth and no intimacy. Father, Creator, bless over my thoughts to and for you. That they are clear with intent and not just fillers. Guide me in deepening my need for you, so that I am so hungry and thirsty for you that I don't seek anyone else to keep me hydrated and fed.

I love you Amen

Prayer of the Day

Father, please bless over this day. There is a sense of urgency and anxiousness in us all. Help us to remember that prayers should replace anxiousness. Calm our thoughts and our actions. I am deeply concerned with the state of the world. We are more focused on religion than being good human beings. Spirituality is the awareness of something/someone larger than us. For some, spirituality is too broad. For me, spirituality leaves us open for others experiences, which keeps us connected. It teaches us not to "tolerate", but to appreciate our differences. Bless over me that I continue to serve my purpose and that I am empathetic and gracious as you have been with me. Amen Ashe

Prayer of the Day

Creator
I come to you humble, vulnerable and surrendering. You have always been faithful to me. Loyal and consistent. I cannot say the same. I am sad and heartbroken, and my prayers are clouded. I ask you to carry me and guide because my choices and movement are my own. I ask that you quiet my thoughts so I can clearly hear yours. I know that I am gifted with truth but right now I cannot hear anything. I need you. This week I have only been praying for others because my prayers for myself have no substance. I need you. I am surrendering and I am free for your movement in my life. No manipulating, no impatience. I'm standing still and waiting for you. Please quiet my thoughts and heal my heart so I am strong enough to stand still and wait for you. I love you, Amen Ashe

Prayer of the Day

Creator, Father, Help me KISS-Keep It Simple Savior. In a world of distractions, usually caused by myself, help me to keep it simple. Help me to love gently, praise consistently, and empathize in everything. I love your presence. I appreciate your Grace. I am thankful for breath. Amen

Prayer of the Day

Father, Creator please bless over me with Presence. Anxiety and worry do not come from you. Help me to come to you first in all things. If I am worrying, please stop me and I will pray. If I am struggling, please stop me and I will pray. When I am happy, please stop me and I will pray. When I am, please stop me and I will pray. Help me to rely on your presence throughout my day. Grace me with mindfulness of others needs. Guide me to serve you in all things because I belong to you first. I recognize that most of my complaints in others may be a reflection of my own. Let all of my suggestions and opinions be filtered through you first. I love you. Amen Ashe

Prayer for the Day

Creator, please bless over us with awareness. Help us to be aware of our presence here on Earth. First you created Light, then you divided the atmosphere from the ocean. Next, land was divided from water. Then the sun, moon and stars and the creatures to fill the sky. Lastly, you filled the Earth with animals.
We, humans were created as the pinnacle. Not to dominant but to support order and maintain your purpose. Help us to honor your gift and take care of all things as you would. I love you and I love my Earth Roommates. Amen Ashe -Syreeta

Prayer of the Day

Creator bless over my day. My heart has moments where it truly stings, and the feeling is overwhelming. I am grateful that the stings are now just moments instead of days and hours. I know that you are moving me forward, and through this and I am grateful. Please bless over all of us that are struggling with a loss. Clichés never work for me but your love and guidance do. I will continue to pray and have faith in your commitment to my well-being, even when I struggle myself. Today I will be productive and proactive in my emotional, physical, spiritual, financial, and mental well-being.

I love you-Amen, Ashe -Syreeta

Prayer of the Day

I'm giving a shout out to my Creator, my God. I am thankful and grateful for your love loyalty. You are my umbrella in this life of rain! You have always been faithful and committed. Your grace fills me. I love you, Amen

Prayer of the Day

Creator,
Bless over us that we are able to stand in our truths. Give us discernment and clarity. We need your patience and continued grace as We redevelop/develop our spiritual muscles! Amen

Prayer of the Day

Creator, I woke up this morning in despair. I know that every trial I endure, you have prepared me for it. I am now ready to fight no matter what. My holistic trainings & remedies are going to be put to use. I am ready! Amen Amen Amen

Just saying...-Look to no one to satisfy your needs the way our Creator does. He is safety, unconditional love, rejuvenation, and hope. It is when we look for people to fulfill these needs that we are disappointed and disenchanted.

Prayer of the Day

God, Creator bless over me with peace and acceptance. That I remember to walk in your presence in all things- my speech, my actions, and my serving. I am grateful for waking up this morning when others did not. I will use the rest of this day to pray for others and not dwell any longer on my own worries. Thank you for your provision and grace. I love you Amen Ashe

Prayer of the Day

Father, Creator bless over my heart. I have learned to live in a flexible definition of being "ok". Today I hurt and I know others are too…for many reasons. Grace us with strength and resilience. Give us peace and mindfulness. Help us embrace our emotions so we can move forward. Guide my life movements so that they stay consistent with my beliefs and convictions. I love you. You love me and everything will get better. Amen Ashe Power-Syreeta

Prayer of the Day

Creator, Love of My Life,
Please give me peace and calmness in my spirit.
Release my anxiousness and indecisive spirit. I acknowledge your love and your gifts to me, and inside of me. Help me to remain on your path. I know my changes are abrupt and many, but I trust you! I know that you move me and those around me. I appreciate your favor and I am constantly aware of your grace. Keep us all protected under your umbrella of truth and authenticity, so I know what's right. I love you deeply.
Amen, Ashe, Power

Prayer of the Day

Father, Creator,
Please bless over my family and friends in need. Help us find prayer before judgement, before meanness, before sadness, before action. Help our first reaction be prayer. Help us be aware of others needs before our egos and pride show up. Show us how to sit in humility, vulnerability, and surrender. Teach us how to be comfortable with receiving even when it is uncomfortable. Grace us with showing loving kindness to others.
I love you. Amen! Ashe!

Prayer-Father

God, Creator bless over this day. Guide my footprints, my actions, my words. Help me honor my purpose. Thank you for your continued grace and mercy. Bless over my family, my friends. Give them clarity and purpose. Show us all, that in the middle of our life storm, we are all ok. The storm is just life and what we think are transitions are just life's movement. Help us live and not just exist. Help us to be still-emotionally, mentally, and physically. I want to acknowledge your gifts and blessings, and honor that you gave me breath this morning when others are now with you-Amen

Prayer of the Day

Father, Creator, thank you for waking me up this morning. I am mindful that someone did not rise this morning. Today I will be present in every way. I know that I am a vessel for you. Bless over me that my words may provide healing. That my touches provide comfort, and that my presence reflects you in all things. Bless over my children that they may be wrapped and protected by you in every way. Please provide peace and calm to my friends and family. I ask for discernment and clarity for the important decisions that I am making. You know my heart and where I belong. Amen Ashe I love You God!

Prayer of the Day

Father, Creator
Today I am praying for discernment and diligence. These two areas have always been a problem for me. I often pray for your clarity and guidance but then stumble over my own interference. Please bless over my recent decisions, and judgement. Please remove the need for absolute control. Having control has been a blanket and safety net for me, but blinds me to the possibilities. I am working on my faith that you will restore, replenish, and renew me financially, spiritually, and physically. Please help my friends and family that are in need of you today. We receive your umbrella of patience and understanding. Thank you for your grace and love without condition. Ashe-Amen-Blessed

Prayer of the Day

Creator, I initially woke up with a heavy heart. No matter what my life has changed. But today I stopped and thought of my love for you. You have been faithful. You have been patient. You have always shown me grace. I trust you. I know that everything happens through you with intention. I trust you and I trust me so my heart can handle anything. I love you-Amen

Prayer of the Day

Creator, I woke up this morning in despair. I know that every trial I endure, you have prepared me for it. I am now ready to fight no matter what. My holistic trainings & remedies are going to be put to use. I am ready!
Amen Amen Amen

Just saying...-Look to no one to satisfy your needs the way our Creator does. He is safety, unconditional love, rejuvenation, and hope. It is when we look for people to fulfill these needs that we are disappointed and disenchanted.

CHAPTER 9
THE BANDAGE

My last coupling exposed the best and worst version of myself. I loved him with so much depth and toxicity. I now truly understand the term “ride or die.” I finally understand that staying no matter what someone says or does because you want them is dangerous. I was frightened when I realized that I would have stayed with him regardless of all my “deal breakers” and “boundaries” being kicked to the side. I did not protect myself at all. The raging thought in my mind that made me finally leave was that my youngest son had a completely different mother and childhood experience than his older brother and sister. I had become a complete fraud in my own life. I coached others on cultivating healthy intimate relationships and healthy personal-professional balance, but there I was in a relationship that tore me at the very core. I eventually left because no one should have to “die” to remain in a relationship. And I was dying - emotionally, mentally, spiritually. The toxicity had eaten me up inside. I was anxious and unsure of my movements with him, with myself. The manipulation had me questioning my normally rational, intuitive self. I felt helpless which was dangerous and reminiscent of my childhood. I didn't feel safe loving him and I no longer trusted myself. While I embraced the intensity of our chemistry and welcomed it with a vulnerability unlike anything I had ever experienced, he ran from it. He told me that I was the "love of his life," but he spent all our time together showing me how little I meant to him.

Being burned changed my very existence. The way I move and speak. I didn't trust myself anymore. The way I love and think. I am a writer, a romanticist, but I had the hardest time watching a romance movie or reading a book. I was scarred deeply. I am capable and willing to love again, but I am different now. I learned that there is never a need for me to blindly trust anyone but God. Everyone else has to earn the space that I share, and any man who wants to know my naked body will need to know God first. He will not have to "pay" for my hurt of the past, but he will have to be patient if I have reminders and need to catch my breath. I deserve that kind of tenderness from a man who wants to share my space.

Last year, I was angry, ashamed, embarrassed, devastated and sad over it. And even though the end of my coupling and my most profound relationship seemed horrific; it has served as one of the most important events in my life. My relationships have taught me so much about myself as a woman, a writer, and a lover. I am grateful and thankful for the men that I have loved. Without the goodness and tragedy of this last love I would have never had the courage to publish a poetry book. I have more depth as a woman, an intimate coach, and empath because of that relationship. When I see him, I don't die inside as I initially thought I would. I don't want to scream and yell or cry and plead. I went through all the stages of grief to be able to move forward.

Denial & Isolation

I could not accept that it was over. I just couldn't grasp that he would be forever gone. I didn't shop at the stores where we shopped at. I didn't socialize with the people who we knew together. I couldn't bear being asked about him.

Anger

Anger - this stage exposed me most. I had never

thought of myself as an angry person. But at night I would dream of us meeting at places where we used to shop together. I would have this reoccurring dream that we would spot each other across the store, and he would walk towards me. When he would get within a couple of feet, he would start saying “I’m sorry,” “I can’t believe I did that to us,” “I miss you,” “You deserved so much better than what I gave,” etc. See, these were all the things I longed to hear. But then in the same dream I would start screaming “Fuck you,” “How could you do that to us?” “I can’t look at your face.” Then we would both start crying uncontrollably. I had these recurring dreams for months. They were nightmares. I couldn’t believe how angry I was…at me! I was scared. I curse for expression but not directly as an insult-like in the dream. I couldn’t believe I was screaming “FUCK YOU” in public. The worst part of this stage was my anger at myself. I was furious with myself. I was so infuriated that I had allowed myself to be with a man who treated me like nothing. It was my most shameful relationship. Most people were clueless and unaware and would not have believed me even if I spoke on it. But I kept my mouth shut because this relationship exposed us both.

Bargaining

This was a brief stage for me. By now only 5% of me wanted him still. I promised God that I would be able to move forward if only God would make him apologize. God must have been laughing at me. I was desperate for some respite.

Depression

This stage triggering my out-of-body experiences. I

would see myself sitting in the center of the bed for hours staring off into space, losing track of time. I skipped eating because my pain fed me. Some days I couldn't even drink anything. I cried too. I cried in the car, while taking showers, during meals, randomly. I cried so hauntingly loud that I would play music or turn up the television, so I didn't have to hear myself. And then I would pass out and sleep fitfully.

Acceptance

Then came Acceptance - this is when I got out of myself and my self-indulgence and starting praying. I thank God for this stage. There are many stages to grief but not everyone completes them. In this stage I was able to see all the areas in which I had gone wrong and the mistakes that I made. I was asked by my beautiful therapist to write out 10 Appreciations, 10 Regrets, and

10 Resentments. I've lived my entire life accepting all damage whether by others or self-inflicted. I had never acknowledged regrets but this time I had one: I did not leave the first time he disrespected me. This is where I realized that everything that had been done to me, everything that had been said, could have been prevented had I honored myself. There is this unspoken expectation of women of color to "stick it out"…no matter what. Because our men have had so many struggles, we need to be extra patient, extra loving, extra nurturing, extra everything. We don't want to be one more thing that doesn't go right for them. What about us? I stayed to prove that I could stay, that I could "stick it out," and that I could be trusted. But all I taught him was that it was acceptable to misuse me. I was so caught up in proving that my love could be trusted that I didn't pay attention to how unsafe loving

him was for me. This was also the stage where I realized that he did not want me. This was the most painful and freeing of the stages. I had been obsessive with analyzing and trying to understand everything that had taken place between us. I wrote down everything that had been said and done between us. Then one day I realized that although he was there, he had never wanted to be. He didn't want me or our coupling. I knew what it felt like to be wanted by a man and that was not it! I was not required to set myself on fire to warm him up. Especially when he just watched me burn. I died a little in each of my relationships. Not their fault, but my own. I chose men who were not available. My adult therapist said to me, *"You have an amazing heart and you never need to offer yourself again. People know what you have to offer and what you're capable of. Let them ask for it."* Damn, she was right! I had never thought of myself as a people pleaser, but I was. I was so busy trying to do things to make everyone else comfortable and happy that I had stopped showing up for myself.

One of my first questions that I ask my Life Coaching clients is, "When did you die"? (Landmark reference). What is that defining moment or thing in your life that changed you forever? Until now it had been me being date raped. I was sure that I could only “die” once but now I know differently. This uncoupling was my "when I died" moment. My deep love for this person shook all that I held dear. In my pain and devastation, I was introduced to my deepest self. That, I will never forget or regret.

I read Nikita Gill’s poem - *The Way Damaged People Love*. I realized as I was finishing Burn Thursday,

Nikita was not just talking about the men I had been coupled with, she was also talking about me. I had been damaged too…deeply. I had spent my entire life trying to outrun the next disaster. My consequences were anxiety, high blood pressure, and a plethora of emotional and mental issues that had manifested themselves into ailments. One evening I sat in the hospital ER because my anxiety and blood pressure was so uncontrolled. I was told that I would die if I didn't immediately change my lifestyle. I kept thinking about when I wrote my eulogy for a psych class assignment 8 years prior. My cause of death was a heart attack. And here I was 8 years later knowing that I was fulfilling my eulogy's cause of death. It was the most painful moment because I realized how careless I had been with myself. I was a human match and it was time for me to light a fire under my own ass instead of watching shit burn! So, I decided to start showing up for myself. It has been the most terrifying decision of my life. The accountability, discipline, and prayers it takes daily not to sabotage myself will be a lifelong battle.

I had an interesting conversation with a man who is dear to me. He is the one who "lit a fire under my ass." He told me that I needed to be still and recognize my placement in this world. He said that I may be successful with helping and supporting others in their relationships, but I was unsuccessful in my own. He said that I needed to work on being still. I wanted to throw out some F-Bombs and hang up the phone with him, but I sat on my bed and listened to him check me. I learned through him how often I don't keep my word. I also learned how much I don't show up for myself trying to show up for others. This conversation with him helped me understand that my last coupling was a reflection of some of the ugly that existed in me. I was so used to just surviving, I didn't realized that I was an imposter too. My intention in life has always been to serve and to create comfort and happiness for others, often breaking myself in the process - financially, emotionally, mentally. This man that I speak of is truly teaching me the art of stillness.

Again, this is not an autobiography or even a kiss and tell. It is my self-indulgent closure to the end of my love stories with men and the beginning of my love story with God and myself. Solely leaning on God for my needs is a learning process. As with all my relationships, I constantly get in the way. I am learning to pray first, then be still for discernment. I smile every time I think of being still. It is a conscious effort on my part. My old way of praying included a prayer, then me "assisting" God with what I prayed about. How very arrogant of me. I found myself basically bargaining with God. I have always known when it's time to make changes, but I try to bargain for time. I now have a prayer closet. I am working on going inside of my closet multiple times a day. God is my nucleus and first love now.

I have had an equal amount of traumatic and beautiful moments happen. But the richness of my life sits right in the middle. I realized that I can create from my experiences - dance, poetry, stories, coaching…this book. I am standing in the middle from now on. I made a choice to show up for myself - emotionally, mentally, financially, and professionally.

I couldn't finish this book until I forgave him, the others, and myself. I released all my shame, embarrassment, and devastation of my failed relationships. I have kept some of my writings for myself, but you now have the most vulnerable part of me in your hands. There is no way to review this book or any other poetry book. Some of these poems are vulgar, juvenile to say the least. How do you review another person's feelings and thoughts? *"Syreeta, you will be okay..." "Syreeta, you will be okay..." "Syreeta, you will be okay..."* I keep hearing Kathleen as I pen my heart. This is how I felt. This is some of what I wrote, and it was time to get it out of me... and now I'm okay.

Burn Thursday

ABOUT THE AUTHOR

Syreeta Brown is a Heart Centered Entrepreneur. She is the mother of three-two young adults and a teen. She believes in following her passions professionally and multiple streams of income. She is a Writer, Wholistic Life Coach, CHO, and Professional dancer but on even given day she moonlights as an Aging Specialist, Behavior Instructor, Mindfulness Practitioner, Choreographer, Medical Assistant, and is adding End of Life Care Doula to her Occupational repertoires.

She enjoys obnoxious family game nights, dancing, diffusing with essential oils and in her creative time, she makes whipped shea butters, natural household products, jewelry, and wellness remedies. She is passionate about intimacy and aging coaching Although she has a filthy mind and a deep weakness for writing romance, Burn Thursday is her first published book. Look forward to publications of romance novels, inspirational books, and children's stories.

If you want to keep up with Syreeta's shenanigans, please visit and join her social media and online community.

www.syreetabrown.com

FB-Deep Sigh with Syreeta Brown-@coachsyreeta

FB-@Burnthursday

Instagram-burnthursday

Tiktok-Burnthursday

Or join her email list at syreetabrown@gmail.com.

Fun prizes given away every month!

I would like to thank you for reading Burn Thursday. I appreciate you for believing in me enough to purchase a book. If you love what you read, please go back to Amazon, and purchase books for your family and friends and write me a review.

MORE ACKNOWLEDGEMENTS

To all of my older cousins Patrick, Shawn, Kim, and A.A., Satin, Santini, Somal, Janice, Frankie, and Terrell, and younger cousins, Lionel, Larry Jr., Lance, Blake, Blair, V.J, Holland, Mason, Brooklyn, Reign, and Phoenix, and my Auntie J.J, and Uncle Keith. Thank you for the adventures and distraction of our childhood, and adult love. I LOVE YOU ALL SO MUCH!

I love you Auntie Kathy and Uncle Vic, and Auntie Laura and Uncle Larry. Thank you for looking out for us.

Thank you to Pumpkin, Auntie Brenda, Aaron and Audrey for showing up for us when my mama was too sick. Pumpkin, thank you for teaching me how to "carry myself". You made me take a make-up class at Fashion Fair, always spoke about proper etiquette, taught me how to take care of my hair, and how to accessorize. I am grateful that you taught me how to take to choose clothes for myself, and how to have pride in the way that I present myself to the world.

Thank you, Raymond. You were my first childhood best friend. I have known you longer than any other friend. I am grateful for our reconnection, sharing, and healing through our poetry and talks.

Thank you to Tynisha from World Financial Group and Chris and Paula from Legal Shield for introducing me to multiple streams of income to support my business endeavors!

To my Queen Gina, you have been one my favorite people from day one. Middle School to High School, and now grown ass women. You have always been Down to Clown and Down for this Brown. No matter what I am passionate about, or attempt to try, you offer your support verbally, and monetarily. I could never eloquently express my gratitude, and deep love for you. We have been through it and survived girlfriend! And I love you Steven for loving my girl. You are a special man.

Thank you to all my girls in my Dance company/world- Vic, Porsche, Candace, Liz, Adam, Christina, Jennica, Jessica, Mellie Mel, Tatiana, Elisa, Yadi, Ashleey, Phylise, Mr. Powell, Shannon, and Ms. Manzo. Dance allowed me to put my heart into movements. Thank you for the laughs and performances! Shaka, thank you, for coming through me when I needed to take a vision out of my head, and put it to drums and movement! Tawnya and William, thank you for studio time at Lyte.

Thank you, Michelle R. and Marie F., for always checking in, and for our girl dates. You soothed my soul!

Jay, I love you to the moon and back cousin. Thank you for our talks and laughs.

Jay R., you are my brother from another mother. I love you deeply. Thank you for supporting and encouraging me in all things. You are the best Godfather to my kids.

To my other brothers and sister-Evan B. Evan P., Egypt,

and Ebony-I love you all and I look forward to seeing you more often and having you as a part of my life.

Thank you to my Yogaworks family, another part of my self-care was getting my restorative and therapeutic yoga on! Thank you, Ladies!

Anna Apple, you make me laugh. I love your heart. Anna, Karese, and Kameshia, thank you for your morning love, and encouragement and sharing pictures of your gorgeous babies!

I would also like to thank a few previous Supervisors. Your bully style management and incompetent leadership skills propelled me the most. I knew that I had to start showing up for myself in my business ventures so I would never have to endure unfair treatment in the workplace again!

Thank you to my old co-workers that came into my office for hugs and morning love. You are greatly missed!

Donna, I appreciated your pep talks and prayers. Thank you for reminding me that I am a child of God, first and foremost, and that God don't like ugly!

Thank you, Nadia, for trying to support and show up for me!

Thank you to Holli, Tina, Kari, Pam, and Sue for providing me professional and personal support.

Mila, you are my heart! Thank you for our pow-wows and talk downs. I am eternally grateful for your presence in my life. You always provide me with objectiveness and call me out on my shit! My mental and emotional well-being is because of our sessions.

Reese, thank you for girlfriend time in the pool and our Ross dates. You inspire me to travel the world!

Thank you to Blanca, CVE, Chris, and Marcie for putting up with me and helping me stay housed while I was trying to figure it all out.

Thank you to book cover photographers-Porsche and Lamont. I love watching you live your best life son. Traveling and choosing your passion professionally. Porsche, I can’t wait to see you as your start your business!

Thank you to the Humphreys for coming into my life when I needed a blessing. I love your family, and I am grateful that you trust me to be a part of it. I love you Lillian and Chuck Sr. You two have been such a pleasant surprise. I love listening to Lillian sing. Thank you both for schooling me on Jazz, Gospel, and Black History. I love your stories!

Shout out to Kortney. You are a powerful man of God. Your surrender will bring you fruit in abundance. Let no one tell you differently.

Thank you to all of my seniors at Palo Verde and Cielo Azul, you have taught me how to age gracefully.

Jimmy, thank you for your help.

Special thank you to my Burn Thursday Crew-Sherry, Tat, Lamont, Lamont Sr., Vic, Otis, Toby, Marjorie, Francisco, Shebur, Meg, and Porsche. I was crazy and you were all there encouraging me. My cup runneth over.

To my Georgie Porgie-I love you dearly. You always remind of who I am supposed to be so that I match my heart with my actions. I love my lunches with you and Joy. You two make me happy!

Thank you Landmark Worldwide for asking me "*When did you die?"* that question freed me to live.

Thank you, Dad for telling me *"do not settle Mija."* This book is me showing up for myself and never settling again! I love you in Heaven.

Made in the USA
Monee, IL
19 March 2020